Weird Facts about the Human Body

Einstein Sisters

KidsWorld

Brain

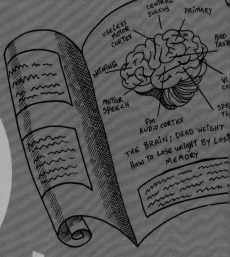

Your brain stops growing when you are about **18 years old**. It gets smaller as you get older.

Your brain is **like a computer**. It sends signals along **nerves** to control your body.

Your brain is pink, squishy and wrinkly. It is mostly made of water. **The brain floats** in a clear, colourless liquid inside your skull.

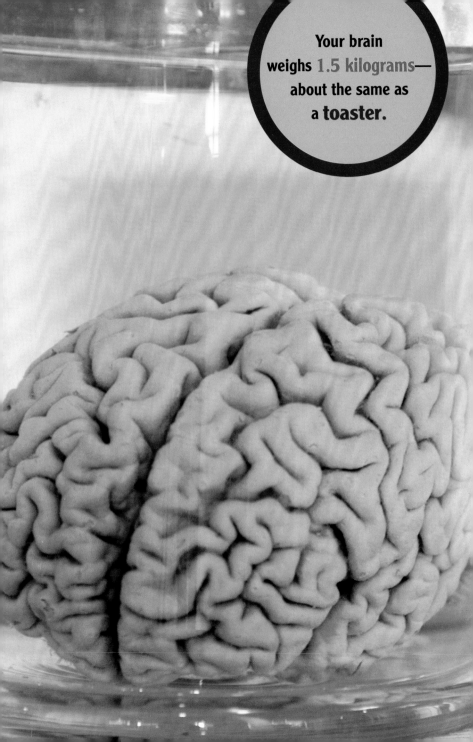

Your brain weighs 1.5 kilograms—about the same as a **toaster**.

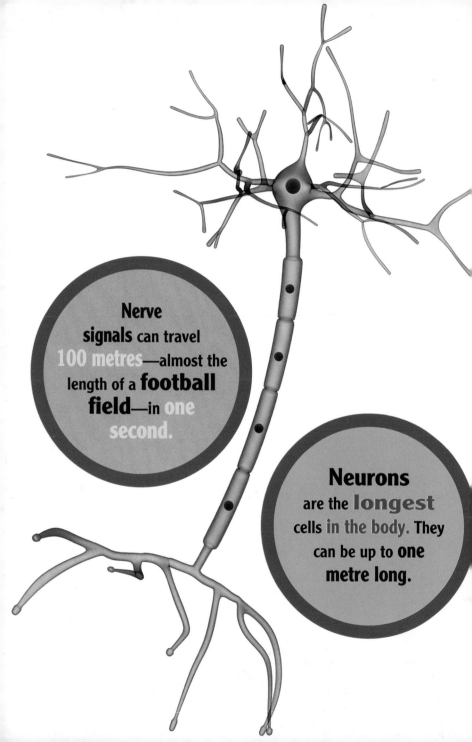

Nerve signals can travel 100 metres—almost the length of a **football field**—in **one second.**

Neurons are the **longest** cells in the body. They can be up to **one metre long.**

Nerves

The **nervous system** is the brain, the spinal cord and **all the nerves** in the body.

The **nerves** are your body's **electrical wiring**. Nerves are made of thin strings of nerve cells called **neurons**.

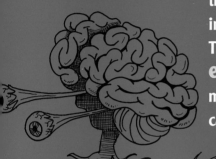

There are more than **100 billion** nerve cells **in your brain**. That is **more** than the number of stars in the Milky Way.

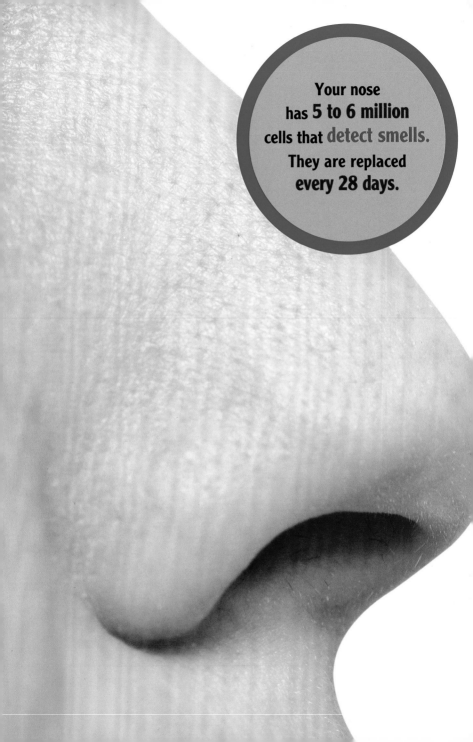

Your nose has **5 to 6 million** cells that detect smells. They are replaced **every 28 days.**

Nose

Your **nose runs** when you **cry** because the tears from your eyes **drain into your nose.**

Men have bigger noses, but **women** have a better **sense of smell.**

People can smell about **10,000** different scents! **Smells help you remember** things.

Hairs in your nose **filter the air** you breathe. **On cold days,** your nose also **warms** the air before it gets to your **lungs.**

Snot

Snot can be clear, or yellow, green, brown or grey. It has greenish chemicals called **"enzymes"** that **help kill germs.**

The **gooey stuff** in your nose is called **"mucus."** Sometimes we call it "snot" or "boogers." Your lungs, stomach and intestines also have **mucus.**

The mucus **traps germs and dirt.** It helps keep your body **healthy.** Your nose **makes more mucus** when you are sick. It is trying to get rid of the **germs in your body.**

Your **nose** makes about a litre of **mucus** every day—that's about **4 cups!** Some stays in your nose, and you **swallow the rest.**

Sneezing

People **sneeze** when they are sick or when something tickles inside their nose. **Some people sneeze** when they go out into the sun. Animals sneeze, too.

You can't keep your eyes open when you sneeze. You also can't sneeze when you are **sleeping.**

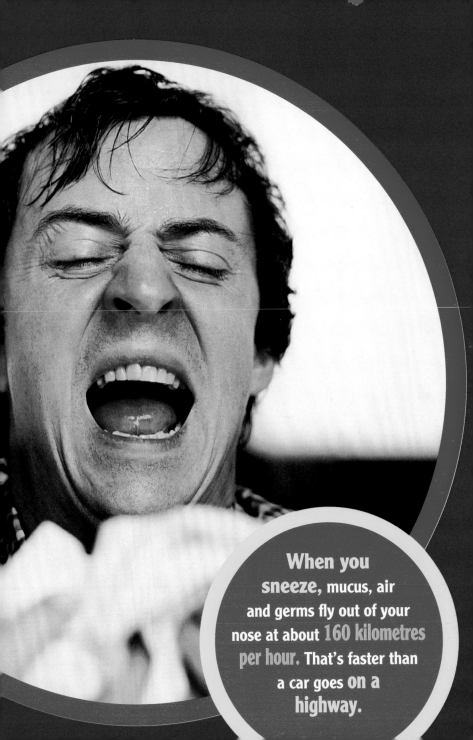

When you **sneeze**, mucus, air and germs fly out of your nose at about 160 kilometres per hour. That's faster than a car goes on a highway.

The smallest **bones in your body**—the hammer, anvil and stirrup—**are in your ears.** All three of them could **fit on a penny.**

Your ears get **bigger** as you get older. They never stop growing!

Your ears hear sounds even **when you are sleeping,** but your **brain doesn't process** the signals.

Earwax helps clean your ears. It collects dirt and germs.

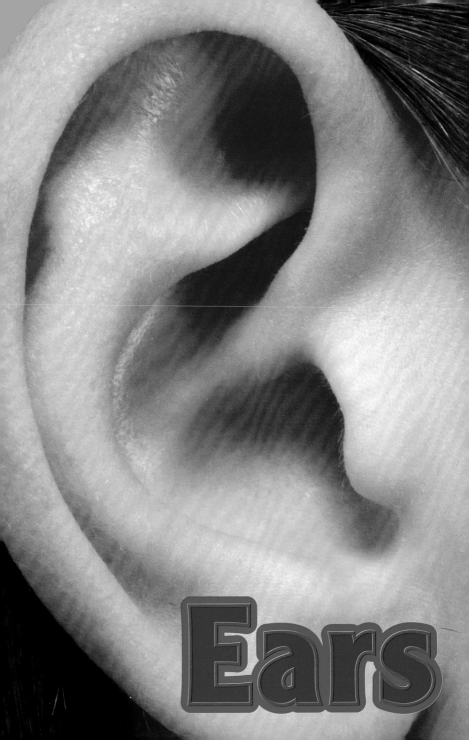

Ears

Eye

An eye **weighs** about the same as an **AA battery.** Your **eyes** stop growing when you are about seven or eight **years old.**

About **10,000 years ago,** everyone had **brown eyes.**

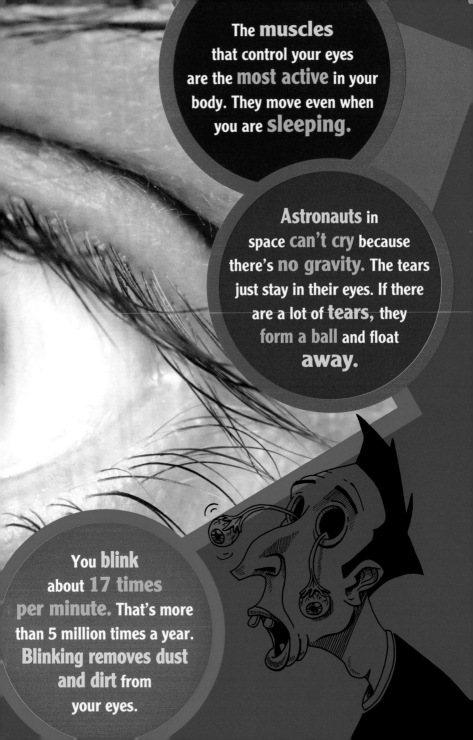

The **muscles** that control your eyes are the most active in your body. They move even when you are sleeping.

Astronauts in space can't cry because there's no gravity. The tears just stay in their eyes. If there are a lot of tears, they form a ball and float away.

You blink about 17 times per minute. That's more than 5 million times a year. Blinking removes dust and dirt from your eyes.

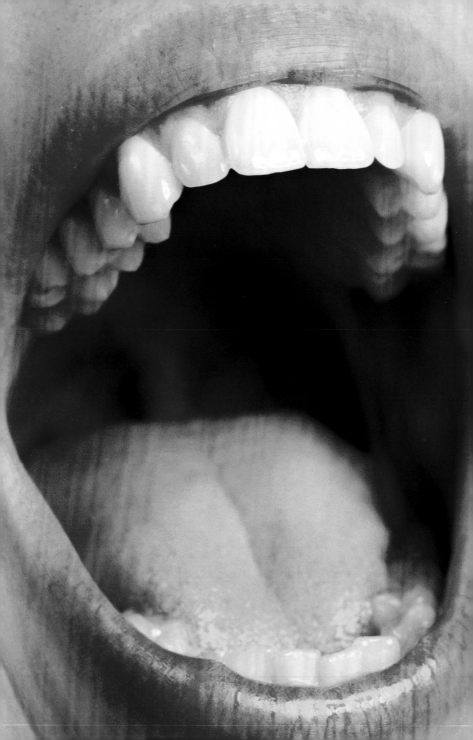

Mouth

Over 500 kinds of **bacteria live in your mouth** (some scientists think there are **almost 1000**). These bacteria make **stinky** chemicals that give you **bad breath.**

You swallow about **295 times** during a **big dinner.**

Your nose, throat and mouth are **all connected.** Some people can suck **spaghetti** in through their nose and out their **mouth.**

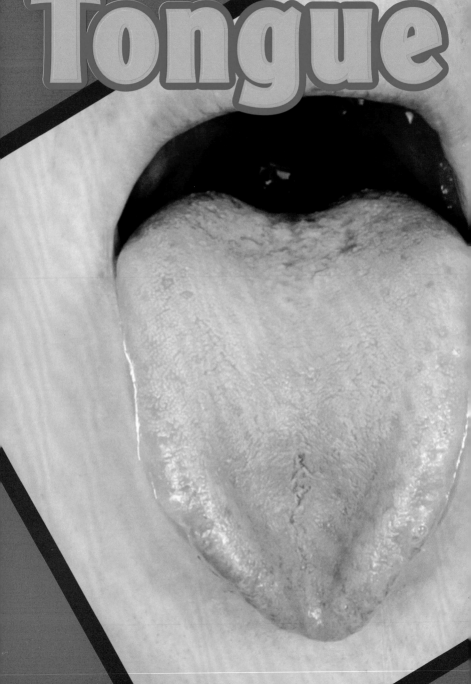

Tongue

Your tongue has about 10,000 taste buds. They are replaced every two weeks. Older people have fewer taste buds, so they can't taste food as well kids can.

Tongue prints are like fingerprints. No two are the same.

Your tongue has **eight muscles.** It helps you talk and eat, as well as taste.

You can't swallow your tongue because it is **attached** to the floor of your mouth by a membrane. This membrane is called the **"frenulum."**

Teeth

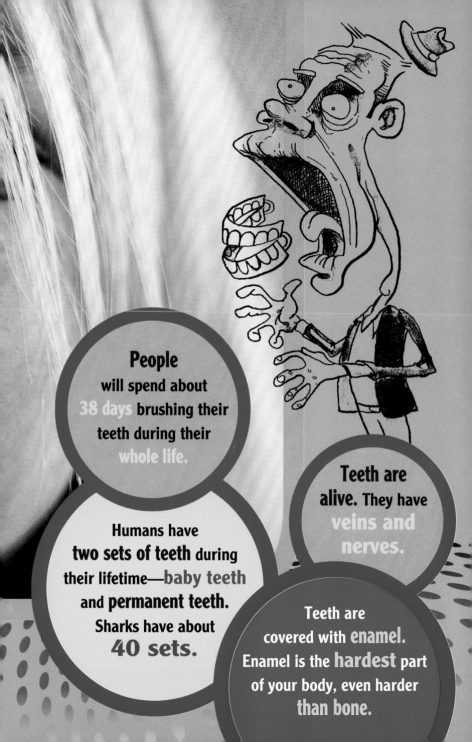

People will spend about **38 days** brushing their teeth during their **whole life.**

Teeth are alive. They have **veins and nerves.**

Humans have **two sets of teeth** during their lifetime—**baby teeth** and **permanent teeth.** Sharks have about **40 sets.**

Teeth are covered with **enamel.** Enamel is the **hardest** part of your body, even harder than **bone.**

Saliva

Saliva, or **"spit,"** is mostly water along with a few chemicals. Saliva helps **break down food.** It kills bacteria and helps stop **tooth decay.** It also begins **digesting** the food you eat and helps you **swallow it.**

Without **saliva**, you wouldn't be able to **taste anything**. Spit helps **dissolve food** so your tongue can **taste it**.

Saliva comes from glands at the bottom of **your mouth**. **Your mouth makes** about **25,000 litres of saliva in** your **lifetime**—enough to fill two **swimming pools**.

Stomach

The **hydrochloric acid** in your stomach kills any **bacteria or viruses** that might be on the food you eat. The mucus in the **stomach lining** keeps your stomach from **digesting itself.**

When you **blush** (when your skin turns red), the **lining** of your stomach also turns red.

In a lifetime, an **average person** eats about as much as **six elephants weigh.**

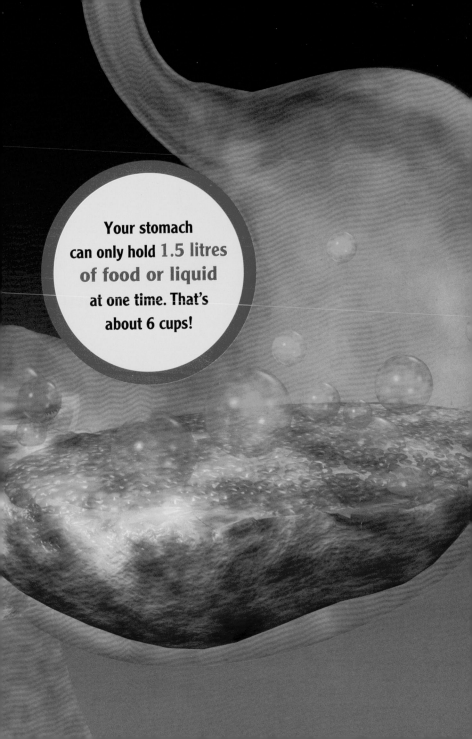

Your stomach can only hold 1.5 litres of food or liquid at one time. That's about 6 cups!

Babies often projectile vomit. The vomit **shoots** out of the baby's mouth with **great force** and travels a couple of metres.

You might vomit if you are ill or if the **food you ate** was spoiled. Some people get motion sick in cars or on **boats**.

Vomit

If you try to stop yourself from puking by **closing** your mouth, the vomit will just come out your nose.

The **green colour of vomit** comes from stuff called **"bile"** that's in your guts. Bile is also really stinky.

Vomiting is also called **"puking," "barfing"** or **"throwing up."**

Burps

The **world's** **longest burp** lasted 18.1 seconds.

Burps are **air escaping** from stomach. The more **air you swallow,** **louder your burps** will be.

Really stinky burps actually contain small particles of the food that you just ate. No two burps are the same.

The loudest burp ever recorded was 109.9 decibels. That's louder than a motorcycle or snowmobile.

Blood

Blood carries oxygen to your body's cells. Red **blood cells** get their colour from iron, which helps them **carry oxygen.**

There are enough **blood vessels** in your body to go around the Earth 2½ times. In one day, your blood travels about 20,000 kilometres—that's halfway around the world.

There are about 5 litres of blood in a human body.

A red blood cell lives for about four months.

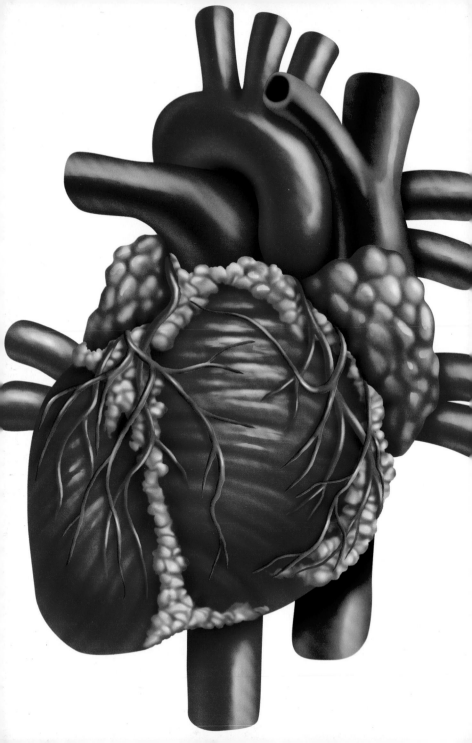

Heart

Your heart beats about **100,000 times** in a day. That's **35 million** times in a year and about **2.5 billion times** in a lifetime.

Your heart will **pump** about a million barrels of blood **in your life.** That's enough to fill **three supertankers.**

Your heart is a muscle. It is about the **size** of a fist.

Most of your **bones** are in your hands and feet. Your hands have 27 bones, and your feet have 26. Your **skull** has 22 bones, and 14 of those are in your **face.**

Your thigh bone, the **femur,** is the **longest** bone in the body. It is **stronger than** concrete.

You have **300 bones when you're born.** As you grow, some of the bones **join** and you **end up** with only **206 bones** when you're **an adult.**

Humans and giraffes have the same number of bones in their **necks.**

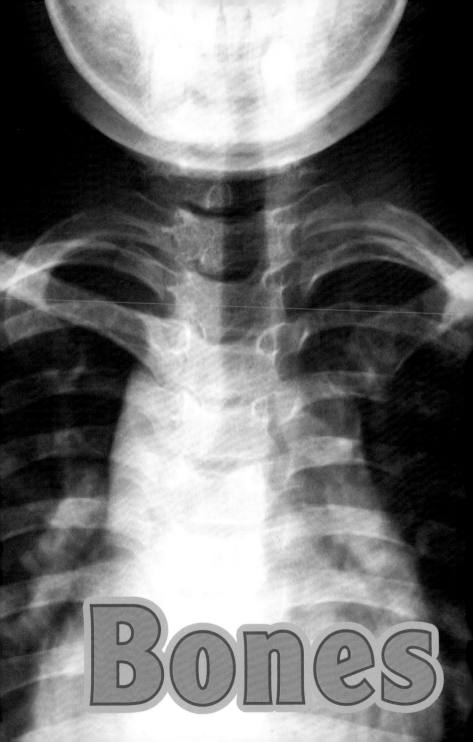

Bones

The smallest muscle is **inside your ear.** It is attached to the **stapes,** which is the smallest bone in your body.

Your **heart** is made of a **special kind of muscle** called "cardiac muscle."

Muscles

Your butt muscle, the **gluteus maximus**, is the largest **muscle** in your **body.**

The muscles that **help you move** are called "skeletal muscles." You have about **650** of these.

Intestines

The **large intestine** absorbs **mostly water.** Food can spend up to **two days** in the large intestine.

The small intestine is about four times the length of your body. It absorbs 90 percent of the nutrients from your food.

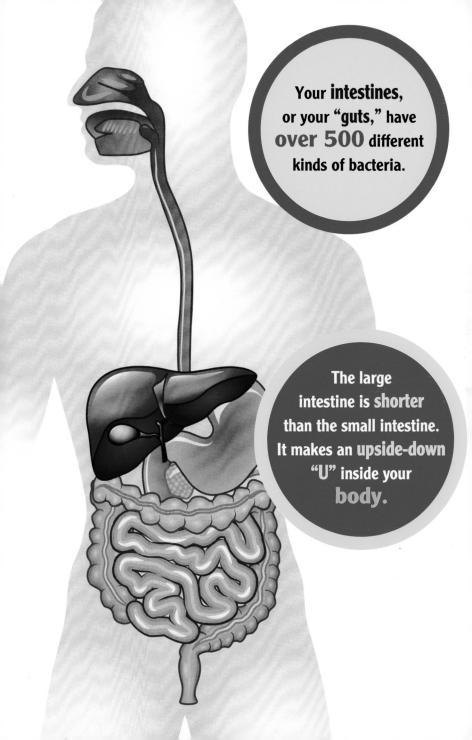

Eating asparagus will make your pee stinky. Eating beets can make it pink.

Children pee about six times a day.

Chemicals from **your liver** make your **pee yellow** and your **poop brown**. The food you eat can also change the colour of your **pee and poop.**

Poop is made of mostly **water**, along with **bacteria**, fats and other indigestible stuff, **like corn.**

Farts

Most people fart about **14 times a day**. The foods that make the **stinkiest** farts are beans, broccoli, Brussels sprouts, **cabbage**, cauliflower, eggs, **milk and meat.**

Joseph Pujol

Farts are made of swallowed air, **chemical reactions** in our guts or bacteria in our **intestines.**

In the 1890s, a man named **Joseph Pujol** performed **musical fart shows. He could** make his farts sound like animal noises and **musical instruments.**

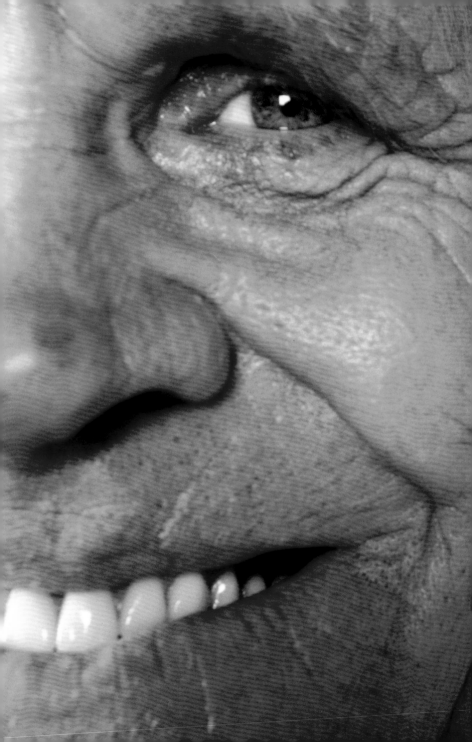

You shed **50,000 skin flakes** every minute—about **50 million a day**—but you don't even notice because **they are so tiny**. Most of the **dust** in your house is made of **dead skin cells**.

Skin is the **largest** organ in the body. **Your skin weighs about as much as a big Thanksgiving turkey.**

Skin is waterproof and keeps germs from **entering your body**. It also helps keep your body the **right temperature**.

Skin is very **stretchy**. When you **get older**, your skin loses its stretchiness and gets **wrinkly**.

Skin

Sweat

Each day,
your body makes
enough **sweat** to fill
a coffee mug.

Bacteria
make sweat smell
bad and gives you **BO**,
"body odour."

You have
more than **2 million**
sweat glands in your body.
The bottoms of your feet have
the most sweat glands.
Your back has the
fewest.

Sweat helps
you **cool off** when
it's hot. Sweat is watery and
salty. When it **evaporates**
from your skin, it makes
you **feel cooler.**

Freckles get darker when you go out into the sun.

Freckles are always flat, but **moles** can be flat or raised.

Freckles are bunches of **skin cells** that are **darker** than the rest of your skin. They are usually **light brown**. Only light-skinned people have **freckles**.

Moles are dark spots on your skin. They can be on **any part of your body**. They can be pink, light or dark brown, black or **even bluish**.

Moles &
Freckles

You get **zits**, or pimples, when one of the holes (**pores**) in your skin **becomes infected.**

The pus inside a zit is made of dead white blood cells.

Warts are usually small, round, flat and **brown.** You can get **clusters** of warts on your feet. These are called "**plantar warts.**"

Three out of four **people get warts.** They are caused by a virus.

Warts & Zits

Acne is when you get lots of zits on your face, shoulders, chest and back. It usually starts when you're a teenager.

Hair

Your head has about **100,000 hairs.** **You lose** about 100 hairs each day, but new **hairs grow** to replace the ones that **fall out.**

Small creatures called **mites** live at the base of the hairs on your body, even on your **eyelashes.** They **eat dead skin cells and oil.**

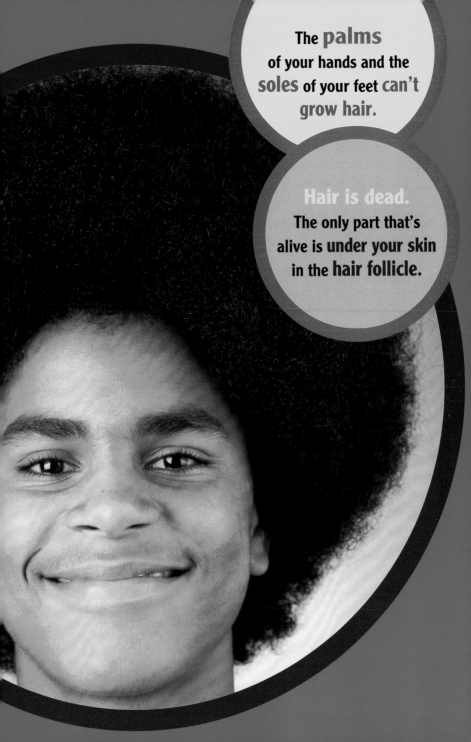

The **palms** of your hands and the **soles** of your feet **can't** grow hair.

Hair is dead. The only part that's alive is **under your skin** in the **hair follicle.**

Hands

Your **fingertips** are the **most sensitive part of your body.**

Each finger has three bones. Your **thumb** has only two bones. Finger bones are called **"phalanges."**

Your thumbs are **"opposable."** That means they can **work opposite your fingers.** They can also move in many **directions.** Your thumbs help you **pick up and hold things.**

Your **fingers and thumb** don't have any **muscles.** Strong bands of tissue called **"tendons"** move your fingers. The tendons are **connected to muscles** in your **palm.**

Nails

Toenails are twice as **thick** as fingernails.

Nails and hair are made of the same thing—keratin. A horse's hooves are also made of keratin.

Primates like chimpanzees, orangutans and gorillas are the only animals that have fingernails.

Fingernails grow twice as fast as **toenails.** Nails grow faster in summer than in winter. The nail on your middle finger grows the **fastest.**

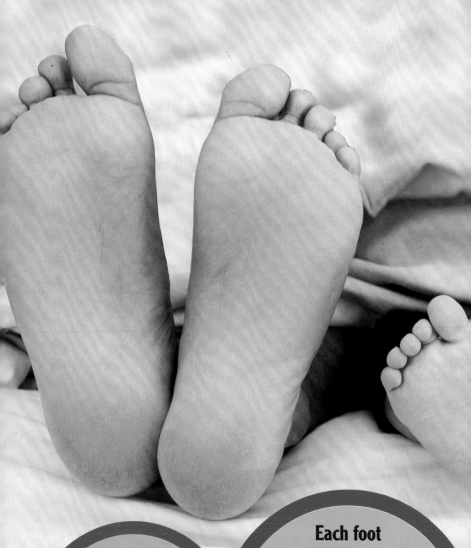

Your foot is about the **same length** as the distance between your wrist **and your elbow.**

Each foot has 250,000 sweat glands. **Sweat and bacteria** make your **feet stink**— sweat makes your feet moist and that gives smelly bacteria a **good** place to grow.

Feet

Most people have **one** foot that is **bigger** than the other.

The skin on the soles of your feet is the **thickest** anywhere on the body.

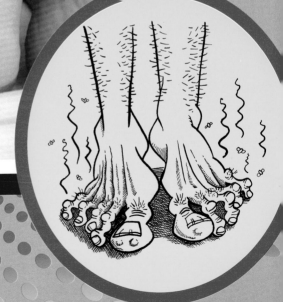

Scabs

Scabs are made from blood cells called "platelets," which stick together like glue, and a thread-like material called "fibrin" that helps hold the scab together.

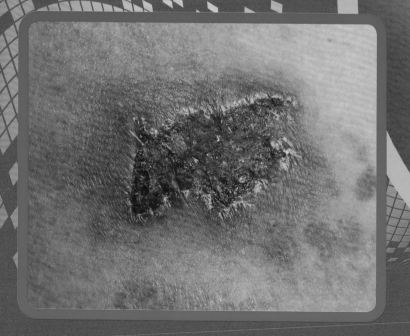

Never scratch or pick a scab. You can get an infection or your skin can scar.

New skin forms under the scab, which falls off in a week or two.

A scab starts to form on a scrape or cut 10 seconds after you hurt yourself. A scab is like a Band-Aid.

Some people think you can make hiccups go away by drinking water, **holding your breath** or scaring the person who has hiccups. **None of these really works, and the hiccups will stop on their own.**

Hiccups

Babies hiccup even before they are born.

A hiccup is a sudden **spasm** of the **diaphragm**, the large **muscle** under your lungs. When the diaphragm spasms, your **vocal cords** snap shut, making the **hiccup** sound.

A man named **Charles Osborne** hiccupped for **68 years** without stopping. According to the *Guinness Book of Records*, he **hiccupped** about **40 times a minute**—that's about **430 million** times!

First printed in 2014 10 9 8 7 6 5 4 3 2
Printed in China

The Publisher: KidsWorld Books

Library and Archives Canada Cataloguing in Publication

Weird facts about the human body / Einstein Sisters.

ISBN 978-0-9938401-1-1 (pbk.), 978-1-988183-16-9 (e-pub)

1. Human body—Miscellanea—Juvenile literature.   2. Human physiology—Miscellanea—Juvenile literature.   I. Einstein Sisters, author

QP37.W43 2014   j612   C2014-903891-7

Cover Images: Front cover: transparent body, Eraxion / Thinkstock. *Back cover:* brain, Creatas Images / Thinkstock; nose picker, Tomasz Trojanowski / Thinkstock; stinky feet, Roger Garcia.
Background Graphics: abstract swirl, hakkiarslan / Thinkstock 12, 34; abstract background, Maryna Borsevych / Thinkstock, 20, 47, 55, 59; pixels, Misko Kordic / Thinkstock, 2, 7, 8, 10, 17, 22, 24, 27, 28, 30, 33, 38, 41, 42, 52, 60, 63.
Illustration & Photo Credits: Julie Dermansky, 3; photographer unknown (c. 1890), 42; Roger Garcia, 2, 5, 7, 8, 10, 12,15, 17, 19, 21, 22, 27, 28, 33, 34, 37, 41, 43, 47, 51, 52, 55, 59, 63. From Thinkstock: andegro4ka, 39; antpkr, 11; budgetstockphoto, 50–51; ca2hill, 60; deeepblue, 26; Design Pics, 16; Digital Vision, 20; Dmitriy Titov, 56–57; dny3d, 4; Eraxion, 30; eriktham, 61; Fuse, 44, 46–47; Hemera Technologies, 52; iliyha1987, 18; Ingram Publishing, 58–59; justme, 40; ngarare, 50; Ninell_Art, 13; Purestock, 25; rabbitteam, 24, 38; Rayes, 54–55; Rob Shone, 56; RusN, 6; saintho, 48–49; samsonovs, 14–15; Scott Griessel, 29; SergiyN, 36–37; SnowWhiteImages, 62; sssss1gmel, 48; stockdevil, 34–35; Tomasz Trojanowski, 9; Vonschonertagen, 31; Voyagerix, 23; wildpixel, 32.

We acknowledge the financial support of the Government of Canada.

Funded by the Government of Canada
Financé par le gouvernement du Canada | Canadä

PC: 28